I0454971

June 2010

COAL POWER PLANTS

Opportunities Exist for DOE to Provide Better Information on the Maturity of Key Technologies to Reduce Carbon Dioxide Emissions

GAO-10-675

Highlights

Highlights of GAO-10-675, a report to congressional requesters

COAL POWER PLANTS

Opportunities Exist for DOE to Provide Better Information on the Maturity of Key Technologies to Reduce Carbon Dioxide Emissions

Why GAO Did This Study

Coal power plants generate about half of the United States' electricity and are expected to remain a key energy source. Coal power plants also account for about one-third of the nation's emissions of carbon dioxide (CO_2), the primary greenhouse gas that experts believe contributes to climate change. Current regulatory efforts and proposed legislation that seek to reduce CO_2 emissions could affect coal power plants. Two key technologies show potential for reducing CO_2 emissions: (1) carbon capture and storage (CCS), which involves capturing and storing CO_2 in geologic formations, and (2) plant efficiency improvements that allow plants to use less coal.

The Department of Energy (DOE) plays a key role in accelerating the commercial availability of these technologies and devoted more than $600 million to them in fiscal year 2009. Congress asked GAO to examine (1) the maturity of these technologies; (2) their potential for commercial use, and any challenges to their use; and (3) possible implications of deploying these technologies. To conduct this work, GAO reviewed reports and interviewed stakeholders with expertise in coal technologies.

What GAO Recommends

GAO recommends that DOE develop a standard set of benchmarks to gauge and report to Congress on the maturity of key technologies. In commenting on a draft of this report, DOE concurred with our recommendation.

View GAO-10-675 or key components.
For more information, contact Mark Gaffigan at (202) 512-3841 or gaffiganm@gao.gov.

What GAO Found

DOE does not systematically assess the maturity of key coal technologies, but GAO found consensus among stakeholders that CCS is less mature than efficiency technologies. Specifically, DOE does not use a standard set of benchmarks or terms to describe the maturity of technologies, limiting its ability to provide key information to Congress, utilities, and other stakeholders. This lack of information limits congressional oversight of DOE's expenditures on these efforts, and it hampers policymakers' efforts to gauge the maturity of these technologies as they consider climate change policies. In the absence of this information from DOE, GAO interviewed stakeholders with expertise in CCS or efficiency technologies to identify their views on the maturity of these technologies. Stakeholders told GAO that while components of CCS have been used commercially in other industries, their application remains at a small scale in coal power plants, with only one fully integrated CCS project operating at a coal plant. Efficiency technologies, on the other hand, are in wider commercial use.

Commercial deployment of CCS is possible within 10 to 15 years while many efficiency technologies have been used and are available for use now. Use of both technologies is, however, contingent on overcoming a variety of economic, technical, and legal challenges. In particular, with respect to CCS, stakeholders highlighted the large costs to install and operate current CCS technologies, the fact that large scale demonstration of CCS is needed in coal plants, and the lack of a national carbon policy to reduce CO_2 emissions or a legal framework to govern liability for the permanent storage of large amounts of CO_2. With respect to efficiency improvements, stakeholders highlighted the high cost to build or upgrade such coal plants, the fact that some upgrades require highly technical materials, and plant operators' concerns that changes to the existing fleet of coal power plants could trigger additional regulatory requirements.

CCS technologies offer more potential to reduce CO_2 emissions than efficiency improvements alone, and both could raise electricity costs and have other effects. According to reports and stakeholders, the successful deployment of CCS technologies is critical to meeting the ambitious emissions reductions that are currently being considered in the United States while retaining coal as a fuel source. Most stakeholders told GAO that CCS would increase electricity costs, and some reports estimate that current CCS technologies would increase electricity costs by about 30 to 80 percent at plants using these technologies. DOE has also reported that CCS could increase water consumption at power plants. Efficiency improvements offer more potential for near term reductions in CO_2 emissions, but they cannot reduce CO_2 emissions from a coal plant to the same extent as CCS.

_____ United States Government Accountability Office

Contents

Abbreviations

ARRA	American Recovery and Reinvestment Act
CCPI	Clean Coal Power Initiative
CCS	carbon capture and storage
CO	carbon monoxide
CO_2	carbon dioxide
DOD	Department of Defense
DOE	Department of Energy
EIA	Energy Information Administration
EOR	enhanced oil recovery
EPA	Environmental Protection Agency
EPRI	Electric Power Research Institute
GHG	greenhouse gas
IEA	International Energy Agency
IGCC	Integrated Gasification Combined Cycle
IPCC	Intergovernmental Panel on Climate Change
MIT	Massachusetts Institute of Technology
MW	megawatt
NAS	National Academy of Sciences
NASA	National Aeronautics and Space Administration
NERC	North American Electric Reliability Corporation
NSR	New Source Review
RD&D	research, development, and demonstration
SDWA	Safe Drinking Water Act
TRL	Technology Readiness Level

GAO
Accountability * Integrity * Reliability

United States Government Accountability Office
Washington, DC 20548

June 16, 2010

The Honorable James M. Inhofe
Ranking Member
Committee on Environment and Public Works
United States Senate

The Honorable George V. Voinovich
United States Senate

Coal power plants generate about half of the United States' electricity and are expected to continue supplying a large portion of the nation's electricity in the future. According to the Department of Energy's (DOE) Energy Information Administration (EIA),[1] coal will provide 44 percent of the electricity in 2035 in the United States. The critical role that coal plays in supplying electricity is due in part to the large coal reserves in the United States, which some estimate will last about 240 years at current consumption levels, and the relatively low cost of this energy supply. However, coal power plants also currently account for about one-third of the nation's emissions of carbon dioxide (CO_2), the most prevalent greenhouse gas. Concerns over rising greenhouse gas emissions and their potential effects on the climate have led some countries to adopt or consider adopting policies to reduce these emissions. In the United States and elsewhere, these concerns have also increased focus on developing and using technologies to limit CO_2 emissions from coal power plants while allowing coal to remain a viable source of energy.

Two key technologies show potential for reducing CO_2 emissions from coal plants: carbon capture and storage (CCS) and efficiency technologies. CCS technologies separate and capture CO_2 from other gases produced when combusting or gasifying coal, compress it, then transport it to underground geologic formations such as saline aquifers—porous rock filled with brine—where it is injected for long-term storage. There are three approaches to capturing CO_2—post-combustion, pre-combustion, and oxy-combustion. Post-combustion capture involves capturing CO_2 from the exhaust stream created when coal is burned at pulverized coal plants, which make up nearly all coal plants operating in the United States.

---

[1]EIA is the statistical and analytical agency within DOE that collects, analyzes, and disseminates independent and impartial energy information.

GAO-10-675 Coal Power Plants

Pre-combustion capture involves capturing CO_2 produced when gasifying coal at Integrated Gasification Combined Cycle (IGCC) plants, which are in limited use in the electricity industry. Oxy-combustion capture involves capturing CO_2 from the exhaust stream created when coal is burned in an oxygen-enriched environment at pulverized coal plants.

Efficiency technologies include more efficient designs for new coal power plants—such as IGCC plants, as well as ultrasupercritical plants—that operate at higher steam temperatures and pressures than conventional plants.[2] Efficiency upgrades can also be made in existing coal plants, such as overhauling or replacing turbine fan blades. Improving the efficiency of coal plants allows them to use less coal per unit of electricity produced and achieve a corresponding reduction in CO_2 emissions. CCS technologies and efficiency technologies can be used independently or in conjunction with one another.

In the United States, regulatory efforts and proposed legislation that seek to reduce CO_2 emissions could affect coal power plants. The Environmental Protection Agency (EPA) has taken steps to regulate greenhouse gas emissions under the Clean Air Act and plans to begin regulating emissions from certain stationary sources, including coal power plants, beginning in 2011. As part of this effort, EPA is compiling technical and background information on potential control technologies and measures, such as CCS, and developing policy guidance to assist permitting agencies in determining the best available control technology for greenhouse gas emissions. In addition, the American Clean Energy and Security Act passed the House of Representatives on June 26, 2009, and would require an 83 percent reduction in greenhouse gas emissions from 2005 levels by 2050.[3] Among other things, this proposed legislation would create a cap and trade program, a market-based mechanism to establish a price for emissions of greenhouse gases, and require additional specific actions to reduce these emissions. For example, section 116 of the bill would require new coal power plants permitted before 2020 to reduce

---

[2]For the purposes of this report, we have defined ultrasupercritical to mean steam temperatures of about 1,100 degrees Fahrenheit.

[3]H.R. 2454, § 311, 111th Cong. (2009).

their CO_2 emissions by half, 4 years after certain CCS deployment criteria are met or by 2025, whichever comes first.[4]

DOE plays a key role in accelerating the commercial availability of technologies to reduce CO_2 emissions from coal power plants. Specifically, DOE's Office of Fossil Energy oversees research on these technologies through its coal research, development, and demonstration (RD&D) program. This program carries out three primary activities: (1) managing and performing energy-related research that reduce barriers to the environmentally sound use of fossil fuels, (2) partnering with industry to advance technologies toward commercialization, and (3) supporting the development of information and policy options that benefit the public. Such information could help EPA in its review of available technologies to reduce CO_2 from coal plants along with other policymakers that are considering climate change policies. In the near term, according to DOE's fiscal year 2011 budget submission, DOE hopes to facilitate the development of CCS and efficiency technologies, with longer term goals of improving these technologies so that coal can remain part of the nation's fuel mix in generating electricity. In fiscal year 2009, DOE's coal RD&D funding was at least $681 million, and $3.4 billion was appropriated in the American Recovery and Reinvestment Act of 2009 (ARRA) for fossil energy RD&D.[5]

In this context, you asked us to review key technologies to reduce CO_2 emissions from coal power plants. Specifically, we examined (1) the maturity of technologies to reduce CO_2 emissions from coal power plants; (2) the potential for these technologies to be used commercially in the future, and challenges, if any, to their use; and (3) the possible implications of deploying these technologies. We briefed your staffs on the results of our work on June 1, 2010 (see app. I). This report summarizes and formally transmits the information provided during that briefing. It incorporates technical and other comments provided by agencies since the briefing.

---

[4]EPA must determine whether certain CCS deployment criteria are met, including whether commercial power plants and other stationary sources have captured and stored at least 12 million tons of CO_2 annually, to trigger the emission reduction requirement before 2025.

[5]Pub. L. No. 111-5 (2009). One of the stated purposes of the ARRA is to preserve and create jobs and promote economic recovery.

To conduct this work, we reviewed key reports including those from DOE's national laboratories, the National Academy of Sciences (NAS), International Energy Agency (IEA), Intergovernmental Panel on Climate Change (IPCC), Global CCS Institute, the National Coal Council, and academic reports. We conducted interviews with stakeholders such as power plant operators, technology vendors, and federal officials from EPA and DOE along with officials from the North American Electric Reliability Corporation (NERC). We then selected a group of 19 stakeholders with expertise in CCS or efficiency technologies to answer a standard set of questions. This group included those from major utilities that are planning or implementing projects using key coal technologies, technology vendors that are developing these technologies, federal officials providing RD&D funding for these technologies, and researchers from academia and industry that are researching these technologies. We asked these stakeholders to describe the maturity of these technologies using a nine point scale we developed in conjunction with the Electric Power Research Institute (EPRI) based on the National Aeronautics and Space Administration's (NASA) Technology Readiness Levels (TRL).[6] TRLs are a tool that is used by NASA and other agencies to rate the extent to which technologies have been demonstrated to work as intended. We also reviewed available data on the use of key coal technologies compiled by IEA and the Global CCS Institute.

To identify the potential for these technologies to be used commercially in the future along with any associated challenges or implications, we reviewed key reports on CCS and efficiency technologies and examined goals set out by DOE, IEA, and electricity industry groups for deploying these technologies. We also asked our 19 stakeholders with expertise in CCS or efficiency technologies for their views on the potential challenges and implications of using these technologies. Finally, we visited coal power plants and research facilities in three states—Alabama, Maryland, and West Virginia—that we selected because they contained projects involving advanced coal technologies. Importantly, our discussion focuses on the technological maturity of these technologies. TRLs describe the level of demonstration achieved for particular technologies, but they do not provide information on other factors that play a critical role in decisions to deploy them, such as their cost, availability of financing, and

---

[6]EPRI is an independent nonprofit company funded by electricity producers that conducts research and development in the electricity sector. EPRI's work contributed to the following report: Global CCS Institute, *Strategic Analysis of the Global Status of Carbon Capture and Storage: Synthesis Report* (Canberra, Australia, 2009).

applicable regulations. Technological improvements could help these technologies overcome some challenges or potential negative implications. For example, novel approaches to CO_2 capture could help to lower the cost of using these technologies.

We conducted this performance audit from July 2009 through May 2010 in accordance with generally accepted government auditing standards. Those standards require that we plan and perform the audit to obtain sufficient, appropriate evidence to provide a reasonable basis for our findings and conclusions based on our audit objectives. We believe that the evidence obtained provides a reasonable basis for our findings and conclusions based on our audit objectives. A more detailed description of our scope and methodology is presented in appendix II.

Although DOE Does Not Systematically Assess the Maturity of Key Coal Technologies, Consensus among Stakeholders Is That CCS Is Less Mature Than Efficiency Technologies

DOE's Office of Fossil Energy oversees research on key coal technologies, but DOE does not systematically assess the maturity of those technologies. Using TRLs we developed for these technologies, we found consensus among stakeholders that CCS is less mature than efficiency technologies.

DOE Does Not Systematically Assess the Maturity of Key Coal Technologies

Although federal standards for internal control require agency managers to compare actual program performance to planned or expected results and analyze significant differences,[7] we found that DOE's Office of Fossil Energy does not systematically assess the maturity of key coal technologies as they progress toward commercialization. While DOE officials reported that individual programs are aware of the maturity of

---

[7]GAO, *Standards for Internal Control in the Federal Government*, GAO/AIMD-00-21.3.1 (Washington, D.C.: November 1999).

technologies and DOE publishes reports that assess the technical and economic feasibility of advanced coal technologies, we found that the Office of Fossil Energy does not use a standard set of benchmarks or terms to describe or report on the maturity of technologies. In addition, DOE's goals for advancing these technologies sometimes use terms that are not well defined. The lack of such benchmarks or an assessment of the maturity of key coal technologies and whether they are achieving planned or desired results limits:

- DOE's ability to provide a clear picture of the maturity of these technologies to policymakers, utilities officials, and others;

- congressional and other oversight of the hundreds of millions of dollars DOE is spending on these technologies; and

- policymakers' ability to assess the maturity of CCS and the resources that might be needed to achieve commercial deployment.

Other agencies similarly charged with developing technologies, such as NASA and the Department of Defense (DOD), use TRLs to characterize the maturity of technologies.[8] Table 1 shows a description of TRLs used by NASA.

Table 1: NASA's Technology Readiness Levels

TRL	Summary of TRL descriptions used by NASA
9	Actual system "flight proven" through successful mission operations under operational mission conditions
8	Actual system completed and "flight qualified" through test and demonstration. Examples include test and evaluation of the system in its intended weapons system to see if it meets design specifications
7	System prototype demonstration in realistic environment. Requires demonstration of actual system prototype in a realistic environment, such as an aircraft vehicle or space
6	System/subsystem model or prototype demonstration in a relevant environment
5	Component and/or breadboard validation in a relevant environment, which could be lab or simulated realistic environment
4	Component and/or breadboard validation in lab environment

[8]TRLs were developed by NASA and the agency began using them in the mid-1990s. In 2002, DOD specified TRLs as the preferred method to conduct technology assessments for weapons programs.

TRL	Summary of TRL descriptions used by NASA
3	Proof of concept test in lab environment
2	Technology concept and/or application formulated
1	Basic principles observed and reported

Source: GAO analysis of NASA data.

DOE has acknowledged that TRLs can play a key role in assessing the maturity of technologies during the contracting process. The agency recently issued a *Technology Readiness Assessment Guide*, which lays out three key steps to conducting technology readiness assessments during the contracting process.[9]

- Identify critical technology elements that are essential to the successful operation of the facility.

- Assess maturity of these critical technologies using TRLs.

- Develop a technology maturity plan which identifies activities required to bring technology to desired TRL level.

Although use of the *Guide* is not mandatory, DOE's Office of Environmental Management uses the *Guide* as part of managing its procurement activities—a result of a GAO recommendation—and its Office of Nuclear Energy has begun using TRLs to measure and communicate risks associated with using critical technologies in a novel way.[10] Furthermore, the National Nuclear Security Administration has used TRLs recently as well.

Consensus among Key Stakeholders Is That CCS Is Less Mature than Efficiency Technologies

In the absence of an assessment from DOE, we asked stakeholders to gauge the maturity of coal technologies using a scale we developed based on TRLs. Table 2 shows the TRLs we developed for coal technologies by adapting the NASA TRLs.

[9]DOE, *Technology Readiness Assessment Guide*, DOE G413.3-4 (Washington, D.C., Oct. 12, 2009).

[10]GAO, *Department of Energy: Major Construction Projects Need a Consistent Approach for Assessing Technology Readiness to Help Avoid Cost Increases and Delays*, GAO-07-336 (Washington, D.C.: Mar. 27, 2007).

Table 2: Scale Used to Gauge the Maturity of Coal Technologies

TRL	Description of TRLs we developed for coal technologies
9	Commercial operation in relevant environment (500 megawatt [MW] coal plant or greater, or about 3 million tons of CO_2 captured, transported, or stored annually)
8	Demonstration at more than 5 percent commercial scale (at least 125 MW coal plant, or about 575,000 tons of CO_2 captured, transported, or stored annually)
7	Pilot plant at more than about 5 percent commercial scale (at least 20 MW coal plant, or 100,000 tons of CO_2 captured, transported, or stored annually)
6	Process development unit at between about 0.1 percent to 5 percent of commercial scale (between 0.5 MW and 20 MW coal plant, or between about 3,000 and 100,000 tons of CO_2 captured, transported, or stored annually)
5	Component validation in relevant environment (coal plant)
4	Component tests in lab
3	Proof of concept test
2	Application formulated (on paper)
1	Basic principles observed

Source: GAO framework analysis based on adaptation of TRLs to coal power plants and conversations with EPRI officials.

Note: We described commercial scale coal plant as 500 MW that emits 3 million tons of CO_2 annually. This is the size of a plant that has been used as a reference plant in engineering studies. Actual emissions from a coal plant can vary based on a variety of factors, including how often a plant operates.

Using the scale we developed for coal technologies, the consensus among key stakeholders we spoke with is that CCS is less mature than efficiency technologies. While all of the components of CCS—CO_2 capture, transportation, and storage—have been used commercially in other industries, such as natural gas processing and oil production, stakeholders generally reported that the application of these technologies remains at small scale in coal plants. Using TRLs, stakeholders generally reported that the largest demonstration of carbon capture in a coal plant was at a pilot scale (TRL 7) or less. Moreover, stakeholders identified only one integrated CCS system in a coal power plant—the Mountaineer Plant in West Virginia—which aims to capture and store more than 100,000 tons of CO_2.[11] This project captures CO_2 from a portion of the plant's exhaust—20 MW or about 4 percent the size of a typical 500 MW coal plant. DOE has announced funding for several integrated CCS projects in coal plants at larger scales—60 to 450 MW. In contrast to CCS, stakeholders generally told us that technologies that improve the efficiency of new or existing

---

[11]While gasifying coal to make synthetic natural gas, the Great Plains Synfuels plant captures and transports CO_2 for EOR use. However, this plant does not produce electricity.

plants have already been demonstrated commercially. For example, a number of ultrasupercritical plants ranging from 600 to more than 1,000 MW have been built or are under construction in Europe and Asia, and there are five IGCC plants in operation around the world, including two in the United States.[12]

Commercial Deployment of Key Coal Technologies Is Possible, but Contingent on Overcoming Economic, Technical, and Legal Challenges

Commercial deployment of CCS within 10 to 15 years is possible according to DOE and other stakeholders, but is contingent on overcoming a variety of economic, technical, and legal challenges.[13] Many technologies to improve plant efficiency have been used and are available for commercial use now, but still face challenges.

Commercial Deployment of CCS Is Possible within 10 to 15 Years, but Faces Major Challenges According to Reports and Stakeholders

While DOE, electric industry groups, and other stakeholders have set goals to commercially deploy CCS in coal plants in the next 10 to 15 years, they acknowledge that these goals present significant challenges. In particular, they have highlighted the large costs to install and operate current CCS technologies. In 2007, DOE estimated the cost to install current CCS technologies was 85 percent higher for plants with post-combustion capture and was 36 percent higher for pre-combustion capture at IGCC plants, compared to comparable plants without CCS.[14] In addition, the large amount of energy that current CCS technologies require to operate—known as parasitic load—reduces the electricity plants can sell and raises operating costs. Parasitic load is estimated to be between 21 percent and

---

[12]There is an ultrasupercritical plant under construction in the United States known as the John W. Turk, Jr. plant. This 600 MW plant is being built in Arkansas and is scheduled to be completed in 2012. In addition, there is also a 630 MW IGCC plant under construction in Indiana, known as the Edwardsport plant. This plant is scheduled to be completed in 2012.

[13]Our past work has also highlighted some of the challenges to deploying CCS. See GAO, *Climate Change: Federal Actions Will Greatly Affect the Viability of Carbon Capture and Storage As a Key Mitigation Option*, GAO-08-1080 (Washington, D.C.: Sept. 30, 2008).

[14]DOE, *Cost and Performance Baseline for Fossil Energy Plants–Volume 1: Bituminous Coal and Natural Gas to Electricity, Final Report* (2007).

32 percent of plant output for post-combustion CO_2 capture and between 15 percent and 22 percent for pre-combustion CO_2 capture. To help reduce parasitic load of current technologies, DOE is supporting research on more advanced capture processes, including post-combustion work on membranes to capture CO_2 that may lower the cost of the current method of using chemical solvents.

In addition, key studies report that demonstration of large scale integrated CCS systems is a technical challenge and is needed to demonstrate the performance and potential costs of these systems. Some stakeholders also reported that additional demonstration was needed to lower perceived risk of technologies. For example, officials from one large utility told us that demonstration projects were needed to build experience with the technologies and to build vendor confidence so that they could provide technology performance guarantees. Similarly, officials from one state public utility commission reported that they considered CCS immature and were unlikely to approve cost recovery for such a project in the foreseeable future. Officials from two financial firms reported that they considered the application of CCS technologies at coal plants largely unproven and they would require additional demonstration projects or technology cost and performance guarantees from vendors or utilities to reduce the risk of financing these types of projects.

Moreover, without a national carbon policy to reduce CO_2 emissions nearly all stakeholders said CCS would not be widely deployed. Without a tax or a sufficiently restrictive limit on CO_2 emissions, plant operators lack an economic incentive to use CCS technologies. Reports by IPCC, NAS, and the Global CCS Institute have all highlighted the importance of a carbon policy to incentivize the use of CCS. In addition, nearly all stakeholders cited as challenges the lack of a regulatory framework to govern the permanent storage of large amounts of CO_2 in saline formations and legal uncertainty regarding long-term liability for the storage of CO_2. In 2008, EPA proposed a rule for injection of CO_2 for geologic sequestration under the Safe Drinking Water Act (SDWA).[15] EPA has stated that it lacks authority to release CO_2 injection well operators from liability for

---

[15]Under the Underground Injection Control program, EPA regulates underground injections of various substances into injection wells. Currently, CO_2 injection wells can be permitted as Class I (injections of hazardous wastes, industrial nonhazardous wastes, municipal wastewater) or Class V wells (injections not included in other classes, including wells used in experimental technologies such as pilot CO_2 storage). EPA's rule will establish a Class VI well for injection of CO_2 for geologic sequestration.

endangerment of underground sources of drinking water until the operator meets all the closure and post-closure requirements and EPA approves site closure of the well. According to EPA, once site closure is approved, well operators will only be liable under the SDWA if they violate or fail to comply with EPA orders in situations where an imminent and substantial endangerment to health is posed by a contaminant that is in or likely to enter an underground source of drinking water.[16] EPA plans to finalize the geologic sequestration rule in fall 2010. Neither the proposed rule nor the final rule will address liability for unintended releases of stored CO_2 that have other harmful effects. However, potential storage site operators are unlikely to assume these risks.

Many Efficiency Technologies Have Been Used and Are Ready for Commercial Use Now, but Also Face Challenges.

Several stakeholders told us that building ultrasupercritical or IGCC plants may not be cost-effective for power plant owners in the United States because low coal prices limit the incentive to build highly efficient, but more costly, plants. Ultrasupercritical plants have higher capital costs because they use advanced materials, which may not justify expected fuel savings. To date, all of the more efficient ultrasupercritical plants have been built outside the United States, where coal prices are generally higher. Similarly, IGCC plants are more expensive than traditional pulverized coal units. According to some stakeholders, if low natural gas prices persist, utilities may choose to build natural gas power plants to reduce CO_2 emissions in lieu of more efficient coal plants.

In addition, some higher efficiency plant designs also face technical challenges in that they require more advanced materials than are currently available. For example, "advanced" ultrasupercritical plants require development of metal alloys to withstand steam temperatures that could be 300 to 500 degrees Fahrenheit higher than today's ultrasupercritical plants according to DOE.[17] From a legal perspective, most stakeholders reported that making efficiency upgrades to the existing fleet of coal power plants was limited by the prospect of triggering the Clean Air Act's New Source Review (NSR) requirements—additional requirements that may apply when a plant makes a major modification, a physical or

---

[16]42 U.S.C. § 300i.

[17]Today's ultrasupercritical plants have steam temperatures of about 1,100 degrees Fahrenheit. DOE has a goal to develop materials to withstand steam temperatures of 1,400 to 1,600 degrees Fahrenheit.

operational change that would result in a significant net increase in emissions.

CCS Offers More Potential to Reduce CO_2 Emissions than Efficiency Improvements Alone; Both Could Have Cost and Other Effects

CCS technologies offer more potential to reduce CO_2 emissions than efficiency improvements alone but could raise electricity costs, increase demand for water, and could affect the ability of individual plants to operate reliably. Technologies to improve plant efficiency offer potential near-term reductions, but also raise some concerns.

CCS Could Help Meet Emissions Limits but Raises Key Concerns

According to key reports and stakeholders, the successful deployment of CCS technologies is critical to helping the United States meet potential limits in greenhouse gas emissions. In addition, CCS could allow coal to remain part of the nation's diverse fuel mix. IEA estimated that CCS technologies could meet 20 percent of reductions needed to reduce global CO_2 emissions by half by 2050.[18] This report also noted that the cost of meeting this goal would increase if CCS was not deployed. Massachusetts Institute of Technology (MIT) researchers called CCS the "critical enabling technology" to reduce CO_2 emissions while allowing continued use of coal in the future.[19] In 2009, NAS reported that if CCS technologies are not demonstrated commercially in the next decade, the electricity sector could move more towards using natural gas to meet emissions targets.[20] Our past work has also found that switching from coal to natural gas can lead to higher fuel costs and increased exposure to the greater price volatility of natural gas.[21]

[18]IEA, *Technology Roadmap: Carbon capture and storage* (Paris, France, 2009).

[19]MIT, *The Future of Coal* (Cambridge, Mass., 2007).

[20]NAS, *America's Energy Future* (Washington, D.C., 2009).

[21]GAO, *Economic and Other Implications of Switching from Coal to Natural Gas at the Capitol Power Plant and at Electricity-Generating Units Nationwide*, GAO-08-601R (Washington, D.C.: June 5, 2006).

On the other hand, most stakeholders told us that CCS would increase electricity prices, and key reports raise similar concerns. MIT estimated that plants with post-combustion capture have 61 percent higher cost of electricity, and IGCC plants with pre-combustion capture have a 27 percent higher cost compared to plants without these technologies.[22] Similarly, DOE estimated that plants with post-combustion capture have 83 percent higher cost of electricity, while IGCC plants with pre-combustion capture having a 36 percent higher cost.[23] DOE has also raised concerns about CCS and water consumption. Specifically, DOE estimated that post-combustion capture technology could almost double water consumption at a coal plant, while pre-combustion capture would increase water use by 73 percent.[24] Some utility officials also said CCS could lead to a decline in the ability of individual plants to operate reliably because a power plant might need to shut down if any of the three components (capture, transport, and storage) of CCS became unavailable. In addition, more electricity sources would need to make up for the higher parasitic load associated with CCS. The National Coal Council has also reported temporary declines in reliability during past deployments of new coal technologies.[25]

Plant Efficiency Improvements Offer More Potential for Near-Term Emissions Reductions but Also Raise Concerns

Because they have been used commercially already, technologies that improve plant efficiency offer the potential for near term reductions in CO_2 emissions. For example, DOE has estimated that efficiency improvements to the existing coal fleet could reduce CO_2 emissions by 100 million tons annually, or about a 5 to 10 percent reduction in overall emissions from these plants. According to the National Coal Council, increasing efficiency is the "only practical method for mitigating CO_2 emissions now" in coal plants.[26]

---

[22]MIT, *The Future of Coal.*

[23]DOE, *Cost and Performance Baseline for Fossil Energy Plants–Volume 1.*

[24]DOE, *Cost and Performance Baseline for Fossil Energy Plants–Volume 1.* DOE officials also said that continued development of CCS and cooling technologies could significantly reduce water use for CCS.

[25]National Coal Council, *Low-Carbon Coal: Meeting U.S. Energy, Employment and CO_2 Emission Goals with 21st Century Technologies* (Washington, D.C., December 2009).

[26]National Coal Council Issue Paper, *Higher Efficiency Power Generation Reduces Emissions* (2009).

However, there are limits in the amount of CO_2 reductions that efficiency technologies can achieve. An ultrasupercritical plant emits about one-third less CO_2 than an average plant in the United States. By comparison, CCS offers the potential to capture 90 percent of a plant's CO_2 emissions. DOE officials and other stakeholders told us that plant efficiency improvements alone cannot reduce the CO_2 emissions from a coal plant to the same extent as CCS. However, plant efficiency improvements can help to facilitate CCS because they reduce the amount of CO_2 that must be handled by the system. Finally, stakeholders' views were mixed on the potential effect of efficiency technologies on electricity costs, but they generally did not think efficiency technologies would increase water demand or compromise reliability.

Conclusions

Addressing climate change while retaining the use of coal to generate electricity will likely require the successful deployment of CCS and efficiency technologies in coal power plants. CCS, in particular, remains relatively immature compared to efficiency technologies, but offers the potential to reduce CO_2 emissions from power plants to a greater extent. The current regulatory and legislative efforts to reduce CO_2 emissions at coal power plants include consideration of the commercial availability of CCS. DOE plays a key role both in its efforts to advance CCS and efficiency technologies toward commercialization and in giving policymakers an accurate view of their maturity. However, because the agency does not systematically assess their development, DOE is unable to provide a clear picture of the maturity of these technologies or the necessary resources that might be required to move these technologies toward commercial demonstration. This lack of information limits congressional oversight of the hundreds of millions of dollars DOE is currently spending annually on efforts to advance coal technologies, and it hampers policymakers' efforts to gauge the maturity of these technologies as they consider climate change policies.

Recommendation for Executive Action

To improve decision making and oversight for coal research efforts, including how technological maturity is measured and reported, we are making one recommendation to the Secretary of Energy. We recommend that the Secretary of Energy direct the Office of Fossil Energy to develop a standard set of benchmarks to gauge the maturity of key technologies and report to Congress on the maturity of these technologies. As part of this process, the Office of Fossil Energy should consider consulting DOE's *Technology Readiness Assessment Guide* to develop benchmarks and reporting requirements.

Agency Comments and Our Evaluation

We provided a draft of our report to the Secretary of Energy and the Administrator of EPA for review and comment. In addition, we provided selected slides on reliability of electricity supply to NERC for comment. We received written comments from DOE's Assistant Secretary of the Office of Fossil Energy, which are reproduced in appendix III. The Assistant Secretary concurred with our recommendation, stating that DOE could improve its process for providing a clearer picture of technology maturity and that it planned to conduct a formal TRL assessment of coal technologies in the near future. The Assistant Secretary also provided technical comments, which we have incorporated as appropriate. In addition, EPA and NERC provided technical comments, which we have incorporated as appropriate.

As agreed with your offices, unless you publicly announce the contents of this report earlier, we plan no further distribution until 30 days from the report date. At that time, we will send copies of this report to the appropriate congressional committees, Secretary of Energy, Administrator of EPA, and other interested parties. In addition, the report will be available at no charge on GAO's Web site at http://www.gao.gov.

If you or your staffs have any questions regarding this report, please contact me at (202) 512-3841 or gaffiganm@gao.gov. Contact points for our Offices of Congressional Relations and Public Affairs may be found on the last page of this report. GAO staff who made major contributions to this report are listed in appendix IV.

Mark Gaffigan
Director, Natural Resources and Environment

Technologies to Reduce Carbon Dioxide Emissions from Coal Power Plants

Briefing to the Senate Committee on Environment and Public Works
June 1, 2010

Introduction

Coal Plays Key Role in U.S. Electricity Sector but Emits Large Amount of Carbon Dioxide (CO_2)

Coal power plants

- provide about half of U.S. electricity (see fig. 1)
- provide over 90% of electricity generated in some states
- account for about one-third of all U.S. emissions of CO_2

CO_2 is the most prevalent greenhouse gas (GHG)

- Concerns over rising GHG emissions and their potential effects on climate have led some countries to adopt or consider adopting policies to reduce these emissions

Figure 1: U.S. Power Generation by Fuel Type, 2008

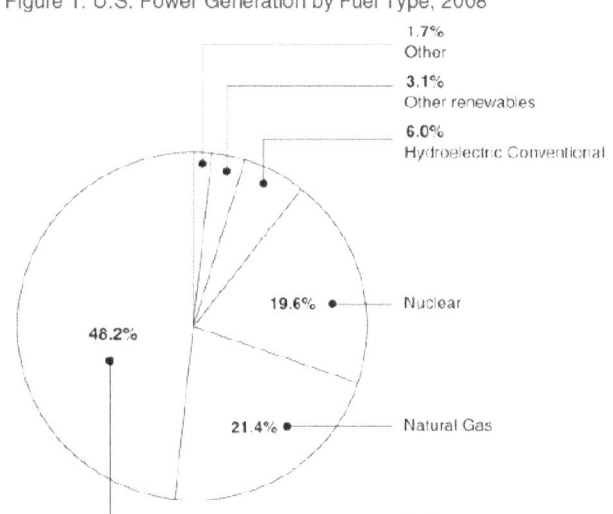

Source: GAO analysis of U.S. Energy Information Administration, Form EIA-923,
"Power Plant Operations Report," January 21, 2010.

Introduction

Two Key Technologies Show Potential for Reducing CO_2 Emissions
from Coal Plants

Carbon capture and storage (CCS) is one of two key technologies for
   reducing CO_2 emissions from coal plants
   - CO_2 is captured in one of three ways (see figs. 2, 3, and 4)
      - Post-combustion
      - Pre-combustion
      - Oxy-combustion
   - Captured CO_2 is compressed and transported via pipelines to
      underground geologic formations, where it is injected for long
      term storage, also known as sequestration
Integrated CCS projects involve all of these components: CO_2
   capture, compression, transportation, and storage

Introduction

Figure 2: Post-combustion Capture

Post-combustion

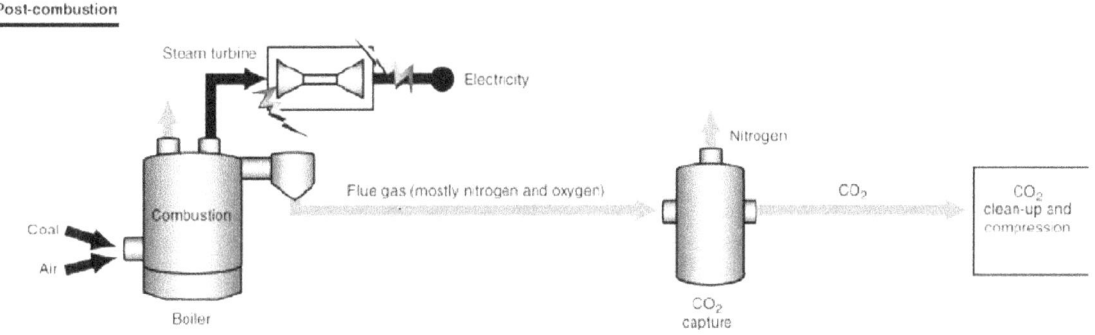

Source: GAO analysis of IPCC and DOE data

Post-combustion captures CO_2 produced when burning coal in air

- Compatible with traditional pulverized coal plants, which make up nearly all coal plants currently operating worldwide

Introduction

Figure 3: Pre-combustion Capture

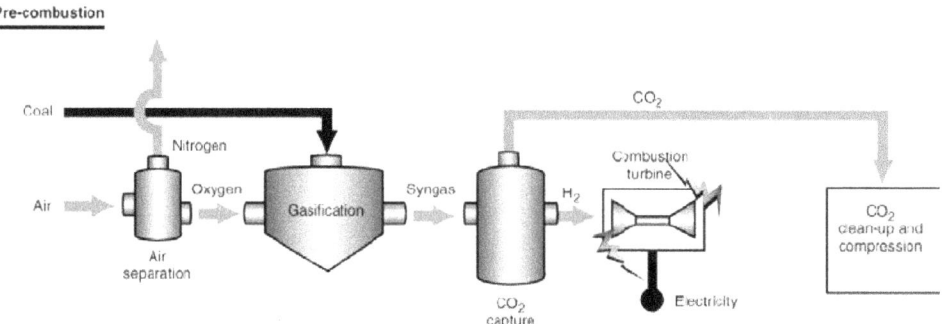

Source: GAO analysis of IPCC and DOE data.

Pre-combustion captures CO_2 produced when gasifying coal

- Compatible with Integrated Gasification Combined Cycle (IGCC) plants, which are in limited use in electricity industry
- The gasification process transforms coal into a syngas, a mixture of hydrogen and carbon monoxide (CO). The CO is then converted into CO_2 and captured

Introduction
Figure 4: Oxy-combustion Capture

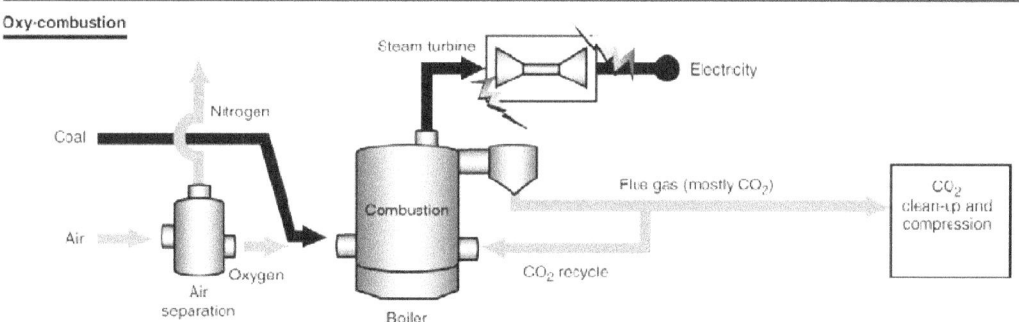

Source: GAO analysis of IPCC and DOE data.

Oxy-combustion captures CO_2 produced when burning coal in oxygen-rich environment

- Compatible with traditional pulverized coal plants, which make up nearly all coal plants currently operating worldwide

Introduction

Two Key Technologies Show Potential for Reducing CO_2 Emissions from Coal Plants (cont'd)

The other key technology for reducing CO_2 emissions improves the efficiency of coal plants (efficiency technologies) by allowing plants to use less coal and therefore reduce their CO_2 emissions

- Existing plants
  - Are about 32.5% efficient on average in the U.S. according to a recent Department of Energy (DOE) analysis[1]
  - Can be upgraded to improve efficiencies by a few percentage points
- New plants
  - Can use more efficient designs, such as ultrasupercritical[2]—which operate at higher temperatures and greater steam pressures than conventional plants—and IGCC plants
  - Can achieve efficiencies of 40-44%

CCS and efficiency technologies can be used independently, or in conjunction with one another

[1]This analysis also found that the top 10% of the U.S. coal fleet had an average efficiency of 37.6%. See DOE, *Improving the Efficiency of Coal-Fired Power Plants for Near Term Greenhouse Gas Emissions Reductions* (April 16, 2010).
[2]For the purposes of this report, we have defined ultrasupercritical to mean steam temperatures of about 1,100 degrees Fahrenheit.

Introduction

Regulatory Efforts and Proposed Legislation Seek to Reduce CO_2 Emissions in U.S.

The Environmental Protection Agency (EPA) is taking steps to regulate CO_2 and other GHGs under the Clean Air Act including

- developing policy guidance to assist permitting agencies in making best available control technology determinations for GHGs that consider the commercial availability of CCS

The American Clean Energy and Security Act, H.R. 2454, passed the House of Representatives on June 26, 2009. Among other things, the proposed legislation would

- establish a GHG cap and trade program
- require new coal power plants permitted before 2020 to reduce CO_2 emissions by half, 4 years after specified CCS deployment criteria are met or 2025, whichever comes first[3]

[3]EPA must determine whether certain CCS deployment criteria are met, including whether commercial power plants and other stationary sources have captured and sequestered at least 12 million tons of CO_2 annually to trigger the emission reduction requirement before 2025.

Introduction

Federal Investments in Coal Research, Development, and Demonstration (RD&D) Aim to Reduce CO_2 Emissions

DOE's Office of Fossil Energy oversees coal RD&D

- conducts research to accelerate the availability of key coal technologies
- partners with industry and others to move research toward commercialization

In FY09, DOE's coal RD&D funding was at least $681 million

In addition, $3.4 billion was appropriated in the American Recovery and Reinvestment Act for fossil energy RD&D

Information on Selected DOE Coal Programs

Fossil Energy coal programs	Technology focus
Innovations for Existing Plants	Develop cost-effective post-combustion and oxy-combustion capture technologies
Advanced IGCC	Develop more efficient IGCC plants and integrate these with pre-combustion capture technologies
Carbon Sequestration	Demonstrate storage of CO_2 in geologic formations.[a] Develop improved capture technologies
Advanced Research	Develop technologies to improve plant efficiency, including development of metals for advanced ultrasupercritical plants
Clean Coal Power Initiative (CCPI)	Provide money for commercial demonstration of coal technologies, including CCS

Source: GAO summary of DOE documents.

[a]Geologic formations being examined include saline aquifers, which are composed of porous rock, filled with brine.

GAO-10-675 Coal Power Plants

Objectives

In this context, you asked us to review key technologies to
reduce CO_2 emissions from coal power plants

Our objectives were to examine:

- the maturity of technologies to reduce CO_2 emissions from
coal power plants

- the potential for these technologies to be used commercially in
the future and challenges, if any, to their use

- the possible implications of deploying these technologies

Scope and Methodology

Reviewed key reports from
- DOE's national laboratories
- National Academy of Science (NAS)
- Intergovernmental Panel on Climate Change (IPCC)
- International Energy Agency (IEA)
- Global CCS Institute
- National Coal Council
- Academic reports

Conducted scoping interviews with many stakeholders, such as power plant operators, technology vendors, and federal officials

From these scoping interviews, we selected 19 key stakeholders with expertise in coal technologies and asked them a standard set of questions. This group of stakeholders included those from
- Major electric utilities that are planning or implementing projects using key coal technologies
- Technology vendors that are developing these technologies
- Federal officials providing RD&D funding for these technologies
- Researchers from academia and industry that are researching these technologies

Scope and Methodology (cont'd)

Reviewed DOE budget documents and program goals for its RD&D program and interviewed senior DOE staff on these

Visited coal power plants and research facilities in three selected states—AL, MD, and WV[4]

We conducted this performance audit from July 2009 through May 2010, in accordance with generally accepted government auditing standards. Those standards require that we plan and perform the audit to obtain sufficient, appropriate evidence to provide a reasonable basis for our findings and conclusions based on our audit objectives. We believe that the evidence obtained provides a reasonable basis for our findings and conclusions based on our audit objectives.

[4]We selected this nonprobability sample of states because they contained projects involving advanced coal technologies.

Results in Brief

DOE does not systematically assess the maturity of key coal technologies, but we found consensus among stakeholders that CCS is less mature than efficiency technologies

Commercial deployment of these technologies is contingent on overcoming economic, technical, and legal challenges

CCS technologies offer more potential to reduce CO_2 emissions than efficiency improvements alone, and both could have cost and other effects

Objective 1: Maturity of Key Technologies
DOE Does Not Systematically Assess their Maturity, but We Found
Consensus that CCS Is Less Mature than Efficiency Technologies

DOE does not systematically assess the maturity of key coal technologies,
although tools for doing so are available

- DOE does not systematically assess maturity of key coal technologies
- Other agencies charged with developing technologies use Technology
  Readiness Levels (TRL) to characterize technologies' maturity[5]
- DOE acknowledges TRLs as key practice in contracting, and some
  DOE offices use this tool for other technology programs

We found consensus among stakeholders that CCS technologies are less
mature than efficiency technologies in coal plants

- Key aspects of CCS for use in coal plants still under development
- Efficiency technologies in commercial use

[5]TRLs are used to gauge technology maturity and use a 9 point scale to rate the extent to which technologies have been demonstrated to work as
intended.

Objective 1: Maturity of Key Technologies

DOE Does Not Systematically Assess Maturity of Key Coal
Technologies

Federal standards for internal control require agency managers to compare
actual program performance to planned or expected results and analyze
significant differences

DOE's Office of Fossil Energy does not systematically assess the maturity of
key coal technologies as they progress toward commercialization

- The agency does not use a standard set of benchmarks or terms to describe
the maturity of technologies
- DOE's goals for advancing these technologies sometimes use terms that are
not well defined
- DOE officials reported that individual programs are aware of the maturity of
technologies, but we found the agency does not formally report on the maturity
of these technologies as they progress to commercial scale

Lack of an assessment or benchmarks limits

- DOE's ability to provide a clear picture of the maturity of these technologies to
policymakers, utility officials, and others
- Congressional and other oversight of the hundreds of millions DOE is spending
on these technologies
- Policymakers' ability to assess the maturity of CCS and the resources that
might be needed to achieve commercial deployment

Objective 1: Maturity of Key Technologies

Other Agencies Charged with Developing Technologies use TRLs to
Characterize Technologies' Maturity

TRLs were developed by
National Aeronautics and
Space Administration (NASA),
and the agency began using
them in the mid 1990s

In 2002, Department of Defense
(DOD) specified TRLs as
preferred method to conduct
technology assessments of
weapons programs

TRLs provide a standardized
terminology to rank and
describe maturity of
technologies on a scale of 1 to
9

TRL	Summary of TRL descriptions used by NASA
9	Actual system "flight proven" through successful mission operations under operational mission conditions
8	Actual system completed and "flight qualified" through test and demonstration. Examples include developmental test and evaluation of the system in its intended weapons system to see if it meets design specifications
7	System prototype demonstration in realistic environment. Requires demonstration of actual system prototype in a realistic environment, such as an aircraft vehicle or space
6	System/subsystem model or prototype demonstration in a relevant environment
5	Component and/or breadboard validation in a relevant environment, which could be lab or simulated realistic environment
4	Component and/or breadboard validation in lab environment
3	Proof of concept in lab environment
2	Technology concept and/or application formulated
1	Basic principles observed and reported

Source: GAO analysis of NASA data.

Objective 1: Maturity of Key Technologies

DOE Has Acknowledged TRLs as Key Practice in Contracting, and Some DOE Offices are Using This Tool

DOE's *Technology Readiness Assessment Guide* lays out three key steps in making a technology readiness assessment during the contracting process[6]

- Identify critical technology elements that are essential to successful operation of the facility
- Assess maturity of these critical technologies using TRLs
- Develop a technology maturity plan which identifies activities required to bring technology to desired TRL level
  - Describes current state of technology
  - Describes schedule and budget to move technology to necessary readiness level

Use of the *Guide* is not mandatory

DOE offices have begun to use the *Guide* or TRLs

- Office of Environmental Management uses the *Guide* as part of managing its procurement activities—a result of a GAO recommendation
- Office of Nuclear Energy has begun using TRLs to measure and communicate risks associated with using critical technologies in a novel way
- National Nuclear Security Administration has used TRLs recently as well

[6]DOE, *Technology Readiness Assessment Guide*, DOE G413.3-4, (Washington D.C., Oct. 12, 2009).

Objective 1: Maturity of Key Technologies
We Asked Stakeholders With Expertise in Technologies to Gauge
Maturity Using a Scale Based on TRLs

In the absence of a DOE assessment of maturity, we developed a scale for coal technologies based on TRLs in consultation with the Electric Power Research Institute (EPRI), which used a similar approach recently[7]

GAO has used TRLs to gauge the maturity of technologies

TRL	Description of TRLs we developed for coal technologies
9	**Commercial operation** in relevant environment (500 megawatt [MW] coal plant or greater, or about 3 million tons of CO_2 captured, transported, or stored annually)[a]
8	**Demonstration** at more than 25% commercial scale (at least 125 MW coal plant, or about 575,000 tons of CO_2 captured, transported, or stored annually)
7	**Pilot scale** at more than about 5% commercial scale (at least 20 MW coal plant, or 100,000 tons of CO_2 captured, transported, or stored annually)
6	**Process development unit** at between about 0.1% to 5% of commercial scale (between about 0.5 MW and 20 MW coal plant, or between about 3,000 and 100,000 tons of CO_2 captured, transported, or stored annually)
5	Component validation in relevant environment (coal plant)
4	Component tests in lab
3	Proof of concept test
2	Application formulated (on paper)
1	Basic principles observed

[a] Actual CO_2 emissions can vary based on several factors, including how often a plant operates.

[7]EPRI is an independent nonprofit company funded by electricity producers that conducts research and development in the electricity sector. EPRI's work was part of the following report: Global CCS Institute, *Strategic Analysis of the Global Status of Carbon Capture and Storage: Synthesis Report* (Canberra, Australia, 2009).

Objective 1: Maturity of CCS Technologies

Components of CCS Widely Used in Other Industries, and a Few Integrated CCS Projects Are Operating

CO_2 capture widely used in natural gas and chemical industries
- CO_2 captured while refining natural gas
- CO_2 captured when gasifying coal to make chemical products such as fertilizer, hydrogen, and synthetic natural gas

CO_2 transported and injected for enhanced oil recovery (EOR) for over 35 years
- CO_2 injected underground to help increase amount of oil recovered
- EOR operations in the U.S. inject about 50 million tons of CO_2 annually, about half of which remains stored underground, according to oil industry officials
- EOR highlighted as a beneficial reuse of captured CO_2

There are a few integrated CCS projects in these industries
- Sleipner and Snohvit (located in North Sea) and In Salah (located in Algeria) are natural gas processing facilities
    - All capture about 1 million tons of CO_2 annually and store it in saline aquifers
- Great Plains Synfuels Plant, located in North Dakota
    - Captures over 3 million tons of CO_2 and transports about 2 million tons of CO_2 annually to the Weyburn oil field in Canada for EOR use

Objective 1: Maturity of CCS Technologies
Stakeholders Reported CO_2 Capture at Coal Plants Is at Small Scale

Post-combustion capture
- Stakeholders generally reported largest demonstration is at pilot scale (TRL 7) using our scale
- Largest project taking place is at Mountaineer Plant in WV, which aims to capture over 100,000 tons of CO_2, according to DOE and EPRI

Pre-combustion capture
- Stakeholders offered a range of views on maturity from formulations on paper (TRL 2) to commercial (TRL 9)
  - Some stakeholders said technology is commercial in other industries similar to IGCC plants, such as the Great Plains Synfuels Plant, which captures 3 million tons of CO_2
  - Other stakeholders said that pre-combustion capture had not been demonstrated in an IGCC plant and that capturing a large proportion of CO_2 at an IGCC plant required further demonstration of a class of turbines suitable for use with hydrogen fuels

Oxy-combustion capture
- Stakeholders about evenly split between ranking maturity as pilot scale (TRL 7) or process development unit (TRL 6)
- Largest project taking place is at Schwarze Pumpe in Germany, which is a 10 MW scale and aims to capture about 75,000 tons of CO_2 annually according to DOE and EPRI

Stakeholder views on maturity are generally consistent with a 2009 report by the Global CCS Institute that used TRLs[8]

[8]Global CCS Institute, *Strategic Analysis of the Global Status of Carbon Capture and Storage: Synthesis Report* .

Objective 1: Maturity of CCS Technologies
Only One Integrated CCS Project Operating in a Coal Plant, but DOE Has Announced Funding for Additional Projects

The only integrated CCS project in a coal power plant is the Mountaineer Plant in WV according to stakeholders[9]

- CO_2 is captured from slipstream of plant's total exhaust with goal of capturing, transporting, and storing over 100,000 tons annually
- Equal to about 20 MW capacity (1.5% of total plant output)

DOE has announced funding for five integrated CCS projects in coal plants through the CCPI (see table below)

Project name	DOE award	Project goals
NRG	$154 million	Construct 60 MW demonstration facility using post-combustion capture technology, with captured CO_2 to be used for EOR.
Mountaineer	$334 million	Capture 90% of CO_2 from 235 MW flue gas slipstream on 1300 MW plant using post-combustion capture technology. 1.65 million tons of CO_2 captured annually will be stored in nearby saline aquifer.
Texas Clean Energy Project	$350 million	Build 400 MW IGCC plant and capture 90% of CO_2 using pre-combustion capture technology. Over 2.9 million tons of CO_2 captured annually will be used for EOR.
Antelope Valley	$100 million	Capture 90% of CO_2 from 120 MW flue gas slipstream at existing 450 MW plant. One million tons of CO_2 will be captured annually and could be used for EOR or stored in saline aquifers.
Hydrogen Energy	$308 million	Build advanced IGCC plant that is 250 MW and capture 2 million tons of CO_2 annually to be used for EOR.

Source: GAO summary of CCPI funding announcements.
Note: Additional integrated CCS projects are planned around the world, but not yet operating.

[9]While gasifying coal to make synthetic natural gas, the Great Plains Synfuels plant captures and transports CO_2 for EOR use. However, this plant does not produce electricity.

Objective 1: Maturity of CCS Technologies
CO_2 Compression and Transport Commercially Demonstrated

Nearly all stakeholders reported CO_2 compression and transport demonstrated commercially (TRL 9)

CO_2 is commonly compressed as part of transporting CO_2

There are more than 3,900 miles of pipelines used to transport CO_2 in the U.S.

- These pipelines are primarily used to transport CO_2 for EOR projects in certain areas of the U.S.
- Some of these pipelines have the capacity to transport between 2-10 million tons of CO_2 annually

Objective 1: Maturity of CCS Technologies
CO_2 Storage in Oil Reservoirs Considered More Mature than Storage
in Saline Aquifers

CO_2 widely injected into oil formations to enhance recovery—resulting in some storage

- Stakeholders generally considered technology commercially demonstrated (TRL 9)
- About 50 million tons of CO_2 injected annually to stimulate additional recovery of oil from wells, and about half remains stored in the formation initially[10]

CO_2 storage in saline aquifers still being demonstrated

- Stakeholders about evenly split between describing maturity at commercial (TRL 9) or demonstration scale (TRL 8)
- Two industrial projects (Sleipner and In Salah) have been injecting over 1 million tons of CO_2 annually into saline formations
- DOE's Sequestration Program has 7 projects that aim to store over 1,000,000 tons of CO_2 in the future, and the majority of these projects are to begin injecting into saline aquifers in 2011 or later

[10]According to oil industry officials, the other half of the CO_2 is captured during the process of recovering oil to be injected again for EOR. They also reported that the intention of EOR is to recover additional oil, not to store CO_2, but this is an unintended consequence of injecting the CO_2. The Global CCS Institute has reported that experiences with EOR have yielded experience with transporting and injecting CO_2, but have yielded little information on CO_2 storage and long-term monitoring of the stored CO_2.

Objective 1: Maturity of Key Technologies
Efficiency Improvements Have Been Deployed Commercially at New and Existing Plants

Efficiency technologies deployed at new plants
- Most stakeholders considered ultrasupercritical and IGCC plants commercially demonstrated (TRL 9)
- A few stakeholders considered IGCC plants less mature than ultrasupercritical
- A number of ultrasupercritical plants ranging from 600 to over 1,000 MW have been built or are under construction in Europe and Asia, with one under construction in U.S.[11]
- Five IGCC plants are operating globally, including two in the U.S. with another under construction[12]

Efficiency technologies deployed at existing plants
- Stakeholders told us efficiency upgrades had been deployed at commercial scale (TRL 9)
- About 10% of U.S. coal plants undertook large efficiency improvements between 1998 and 2008 according to DOE analysis[13]

[11]This ultrasupercritical plant is known as the John W. Turk, Jr. Plant. This 600 MW plant is being built in Arkansas and is scheduled to be completed in 2012.
[12]This IGCC plant is known as the Edwardsport plant. This 630 MW plant is being built in Indiana and is scheduled to be completed in 2012.
[13]DOE, *Improving Efficiency of Coal-Fired Power Plants for Near Term Greenhouse Gas Emissions Reductions* (Feb. 25, 2010).

GAO-10-675 Coal Power Plants

Objective 2: Challenges to Use of Key Technologies
Commercial Deployment Possible, but Contingent on Overcoming
Economic, Technical, and Legal Challenges

Commercial deployment of CCS possible within 10-15 years, but
faces major challenges according to reports and stakeholders
- Current CCS technologies are costly to install and operate
- Demonstration of large scale integrated CCS systems needed
to assure stakeholders
- U.S. lacks national carbon policy or legal framework to govern
CO_2 storage

Many efficiency technologies have been used and are available for
commercial use, but still face challenges
- High efficiency coal plants may not be cost-effective
- Some higher efficiency plant designs not fully demonstrated
and require advanced materials
- Improvements made to existing plants may trigger additional
regulatory requirements

Objective 2: Challenges to Use of Key Technologies
Several Groups Expect CCS Deployment in 10-15 Years

Stakeholder group	Goals for commercial deployment of CCS
DOE	Widespread, affordable deployment of CCS should begin in 8-10 years
National Coal Council	By 2020, deployment of CCS in 5 to 7 gigawatts worth of power plants as part of a "pioneer phase of deployment"
IEA	Commercial deployment of CCS should begin by 2025
Coal Utilization Research Council, an industry group, and EPRI	Identifies family of technologies to reduce emissions from coal plants, including CCS and efficiency technologies by 2025

Source: GAO summary of relevant reports.

Objective 2: Challenges to Use of CCS Technologies
Economic: Current CCS Technologies are Costly to Install and Operate

Current CCS technologies are costly to install
- In 2007 DOE estimated initial capital investment costs could be
  - 85% higher for plants with post-combustion capture and
  - 36% higher for pre-combustion capture at IGCC plants, compared to comparable plants without CCS[14]
- Electric utilities not likely to adopt costly technologies without assured cost recovery

Current CCS technologies require significant energy to operate, reducing the electricity plants can sell and raising operating costs
- Parasitic loads—energy used onsite—for current CCS technologies are estimated to be
  - between about 21% and 32% of plant output for post-combustion
  - between 15% and 22% of plant output for pre-combustion[15]
- DOE devoting R&D money to develop novel CO_2 capture technologies to lower the parasitic load, but these remain at smaller scale
  - DOE is funding post-combustion work on membranes, sorbents, and solvents in the hope of lowering the current cost of CO_2 capture
  - Research is also being conducted on using captured CO_2 to grow algae, a potential liquid transportation fuel

---

[14]DOE, *Cost and Performance Baseline for Fossil Energy Plants–Volume 1: Bituminous Coal and Natural Gas to Electricity, Final Report* (2007).
[15]MIT, *The Future of Coal* (Cambridge, Mass., 2007). DOE, *Cost and Performance Baseline for Fossil Energy Plants–Volume 1.*

Objective 2: Challenges to Use of CCS Technologies

Technical: Demonstration of Large Scale Integrated CCS Systems
Needed to Assure Stakeholders

Key studies report that demonstration of large scale integrated CCS systems
is needed to

- Demonstrate the performance and potential costs of these systems
- Gain experience in designing and building systems to help drive down the costs of these technologies

Some stakeholders also reported that additional demonstration needed to
lower perceived risk of technologies

- Officials from one large electric utility told us that demonstration projects were needed to build experience with the technologies and to build vendor confidence so that they could provide technology performance guarantees
- Officials from one state public utility commission reported that they considered CCS immature and were unlikely to approve cost recovery for a plant with CCS in the foreseeable future
- Officials from two financial firms reported that they considered the application of CCS technologies at coal plants largely unproven and they would require additional demonstration projects and performance guarantees from technology vendors to help reduce the risk of financing these projects

Objective 2: Challenges to Use of CCS Technologies
Legal: U.S. Lacks National Carbon Policy or Legal or Regulatory
Framework to Govern CO_2 Storage

Without national carbon policy, nearly all stakeholders said CCS would not be widely deployed
- Without a tax or a sufficiently restrictive limit on CO_2 emissions, plant operators lack economic incentive to reduce emissions
- Reports by IPCC, NAS, and Global CCS Institute have all highlighted the importance of a carbon policy to incentivize the use CCS
- Such a policy driver could help to accelerate the development of CCS

Lack of a regulatory framework for storing CO_2 and uncertainty regarding liability for stored CO_2 are also challenges
- Nearly all stakeholders reported these as large or very large challenges to storing CO_2
- EPA to issue a final rule for injection of CO_2 for geologic sequestration in fall 2010 under the Safe Drinking Water Act (SDWA)
  - EPA lacks authority to release well operators from liability for endangerment of underground sources of drinking water until the operator meets all of the closure and post-closure requirements and EPA approves site closure
  - Once site closure is approved, operators are only liable under the SDWA for violating or failing to comply with EPA orders in situations that pose an imminent and substantial endangerment
  - Potential storage site operators are unlikely to assume this risk
- EPA's rule will not address who is liable for unintended releases of stored CO_2 that have other harmful effects
- Determining ownership of subsurface pore space presents additional challenge

Objective 2: Challenges to Use of Efficiency Technologies
Economic: High Efficiency Coal Plants May Not Be Cost-Effective

Low prices for coal and other fuels in the U.S. may limit the incentive to build more efficient, but costly, plants
- Ultrasupercritical plants have higher capital costs because they use advanced materials, which may not justify expected fuel savings
- IGCC plants are more expensive than pulverized coal units, and there are few in operation globally
- If low natural gas prices persist, utilities may choose to build natural gas power plants to reduce CO_2 emissions in lieu of efficient coal plants

Incentives complicate construction of more efficient plants in regulated states
- Building new, more efficient coal plants faces hurdles
  - State utility commission approval required to build new plants
  - Demonstrating merits of more efficient plants may be difficult
- Fuel clauses may limit utility interest in fuel savings
  - Some utilities can "pass through" coal price increases to customers using fuel adjustment clauses

To date, all of the more efficient ultrasupercritical plants have been built outside the U.S., where coal prices are generally higher

A tax or limit on CO_2 emissions could increase the price of coal and help to incentivize the adoption of efficiency technologies

Objective 2: Challenges to Use of Efficiency Technologies
Technical: Some Higher Efficiency Plant Designs Not Fully
Demonstrated and Require Advanced Materials

Some advanced power plant designs require materials that can
withstand more extreme conditions than those found in
current plants

"Advanced" ultrasupercritical plants require development of
metal alloys to withstand steam temperatures that could be
300 to 500 degrees Fahrenheit higher than today's
ultrasupercritical plants[16]

Advanced IGCC plants require development of certain
components, including more efficient ways to generate
oxygen and improved gasifiers that can gasify coal at higher
pressures

[16]Today's ultrasupercritical plants have steam temperatures of about 1,100 degrees Fahrenheit. DOE has a goal to develop materials to
withstand steam temperatures of 1,400 to 1,600 degrees Fahrenheit.

Objective 2: Challenges to Use of Efficiency Technologies
Regulatory: Improvements May Subject Existing Plants to Additional
Regulations

Most stakeholders said the Clean Air Act's New Source Review
(NSR) requirements limit efficiency improvements at existing
plants

- NSR is triggered when a company constructs new facilities or
  makes a major modification—a physical or operational change
  that would result in a significant net increase in emissions
- Under NSR, permitting authorities establish emissions limits for
  the facility and ensure the appropriate pollution controls will be
  used

Several stakeholders said that utilities could improve their
plants' efficiency but were reluctant to do so because they
feared this would trigger NSR which could require the
installation of costly pollution controls

Objective 3: Implications of Using Key Technologies
CCS Offers More Potential to Reduce CO_2 Emissions than Efficiency
Improvements Alone, and Both Could Have Cost and Other Effects

CCS has positive and negative implications
- A key advantage is that CCS could help meet GHG limits and allow coal to remain part of the nation's fuel mix
- The use of CCS raises some key concerns
  - Electricity costs and demand for water could increase[17]
  - Could affect ability of individual plants to operate reliably

Technologies to improve the efficiency of coal plants have positive and negative implications
- A key advantage is that plant efficiency improvements offer more potential for near term emissions reductions
- The use of efficiency technologies raises some concerns
  - Unlikely to meet ambitious cuts in CO_2 by themselves
  - Stakeholders had mixed views on other potential effects, such as cost

[17]Water is needed to generate electricity and process fuels to generate electricity. Due to the parasitic load associated with current CCS technologies, more electricity must be produced to supply the same amount of electricity to consumers, leading to additional water consumption. See GAO, *Energy-Water Nexus: Improvements to Federal Water Use Data Would Increase Understanding of Trends in Power Plant Water Use*, GAO-10-23 (Washington, D.C.: Oct. 16, 2009).

Objective 3: Implications of Using CCS
CCS Could Help Meet GHG Limits and Allow Coal to Remain Part of Fuel Mix

Key reports have highlighted the key role that CCS could have in meeting potential limits on GHG emissions
- EPRI – Estimated that CCS could help meet 12% of reductions needed to reduce emissions in electricity sector by 41% by 2030[18]
- IEA – Estimated that CCS could meet 20% of reductions needed to reduce global CO_2 emissions by half by 2050[19]
  - Both studies note that cost of meeting these limits would increase if CCS not deployed

CCS could allow coal to remain part of fuel mix according to stakeholders and reports
- Majority of stakeholders said CCS would allow coal to remain part of fuel mix for generating electricity
- Massachusetts Institute of Technology (MIT) researchers called CCS the "critical enabling technology" to reduce CO_2 emissions while allowing continued use of coal in the future[20]
- NAS stated if CCS does not develop, electricity sector could move more towards using natural gas to meet emissions targets[21]
- GAO's past work found that switching from coal to natural gas could lead to higher fuel costs, and increased exposure to the greater price volatility of natural gas[22]

[18]EPRI, *PRISM/MERGE Analysis* (Palo Alto, California, 2009).

[19]IEA, *Technology Roadmap: Carbon capture and storage* (Paris, France, 2009.)

[20]MIT, *The Future of Coal.*

[21]NAS, *America's Energy Future* (Washington, D.C., 2009).

[22]GAO, *Economic and Other Implications of Switching from Coal to Natural Gas at the Capital Power Plant and at Electricity-Generating Units Nationwide,* GAO-08-601R (Washington, D.C.: May 1, 2008).

Objective 3: Implications of Using CCS
CCS Could Increase Electricity Costs and Water Demand

Most stakeholders told us that CCS would likely increase electricity costs

In addition, key reports have estimated potential cost increases

- MIT estimated that plants with post-combustion capture have 61% higher cost of electricity, and IGCC plants with pre-combustion capture have a 27% higher cost[23]
- DOE estimated that plants with post-combustion capture have 83% higher cost of electricity, while IGCC plants with pre-combustion capture have a 36% higher cost[24]

DOE has raised concerns about water consumption associated with CCS

- DOE estimated that post-combustion capture technology could almost double water consumption at a coal plant, while pre-combustion capture could increase water use by 73%

- DOE officials said that continued development of CCS and cooling technologies could significantly reduce water use for CCS

[23]MIT, *The Future of Coal.*
[24]DOE, *Cost and Performance Baseline for Fossil Energy Plants–Volume 1.*

Objective 3: Implications of Using CCS
CCS Could Compromise Reliability

Some utility officials said CCS could lead to decline in reliability of individual plants

- A power plant might need to shut down if any of the three components (capture, transportation, storage) of CCS became unavailable
- Such unplanned shutdowns could impact reliability of electric supply

Other sources of electricity would need to make up for the parasitic load associated with CCS

National Coal Council reported temporary declines in reliability during past deployments of new coal technologies[25]

[25]National Coal Council, *Low-Carbon Coal: Meeting U.S. Energy, Employment and CO_2 Emission Goals with 21st Century Technologies* (Washington, D.C., December 2009).

Objective 3: Implications of Using Efficiency Technologies
Plant Efficiency Improvements Offer Potential for Near Term
Emissions Reductions but Raise Some Concerns

Plant efficiency improvements offer potential for near term emissions reductions
- Making efficiency upgrades to existing fleet can happen much sooner than building new, more efficient plants
- DOE estimates that efficiency improvements could reduce CO_2 emissions by 100 million tons annually, about an overall 5-10% reduction in fleet emissions
- According to National Coal Council, increasing efficiency is "only practical method for mitigating CO_2 emissions now" in coal plants[26]

Plant efficiency improvements alone cannot reduce CO_2 emissions from a coal plant to the same extent as CCS according to DOE and others
- Ultrasupercritical coal plant with 44% efficiency will emit about a one-third less CO_2 than an average U.S. plant
- Upgrades made to existing plants can improve efficiency by a few percentage points, resulting in a decline in CO_2 emissions from the plant by about 5-10%
- CCS offers potential to capture 90% of a plant's CO_2 emissions
- Efficiency improvements can, however, facilitate CCS because they help reduce the amount of CO_2 to be handled by the CCS system

Stakeholders had mixed views on other potential effects
- Stakeholders' views were mixed on potential effect on electricity costs
- Stakeholders generally did not think efficiency technologies would increase water demand or compromise reliability

[26]National Coal Council Issue Paper, *Higher Efficiency Power Generation Reduces Emissions* (2009).

Concluding Observations

Addressing climate change while retaining the use of coal power plants will likely require the successful deployment of new technologies

- CCS, in particular, remains relatively immature compared to efficiency technologies
- Some of the discussions surrounding regulatory efforts and proposed climate change legislation have focused on the commercial availability of CCS technologies
- DOE plays a key role in helping to accelerate commercial availability of CCS technologies and is spending hundreds of millions of dollars annually for this effort
- Standards for internal controls require agency managers to compare actual program performance to planned or expected results and analyze significant differences
- DOE is not systematically assessing the maturity or progress of CCS or other advanced coal technologies toward commercialization
- As a result, DOE cannot provide
  - A clear picture of the maturity of technologies, and resources needed to achieve commercial demonstration
  - Critical information for policymakers as they consider climate change policies

Potential Next Steps for DOE

Develop a standard set of benchmarks to gauge the maturity of key coal technologies and report to Congress on the maturity of these technologies

Consider using its *Technology Readiness Assessment Guide* to develop benchmarks and reporting requirements for coal technologies

Appendix II: Scope and Methodology

To conduct this work, we reviewed key reports including those from the Department of Energy's (DOE) national laboratories, the National Academy of Sciences, International Energy Agency (IEA), Intergovernmental Panel on Climate Change, Global CCS Institute, the National Coal Council, and academic reports.

To identify stakeholders' views on these technologies, we conducted initial scoping interviews with power plant operators, technology vendors, and federal officials from the Environmental Protection Agency (EPA) and DOE. Following this initial round of interviews, we selected a group of 19 stakeholders with expertise in carbon capture and storage (CCS) or technologies to improve coal plant efficiency and asked them a set of standard questions. This group of stakeholders included representatives from major utilities that are planning or implementing projects that use these technologies, technology vendors that are developing these technologies, federal officials that are providing research, development, and demonstration funding for these technologies, and researchers from academia or industry that are actively researching these technologies.

During these interviews, we asked stakeholders to describe the maturity of technologies in terms of a scale we developed, based on Technology Readiness Levels (TRL). TRLs are a tool developed by the National Aeronautics and Space Administration and used by various federal agencies to rate the extent to which technologies have been demonstrated to work as intended using a scale of 1 to 9. In developing TRLs for coal technologies, we consulted with the Electric Power Research Institute (EPRI), which had recently used a similar approach to examine the maturity of coal technologies.[1] Specifically, EPRI developed specific benchmarks to describe TRLs in the context of a commercial scale coal power plant. For example, they defined TRL 8 as demonstration at more than 25 percent the size of a commercial scale plant. We applied these benchmarks to a commercial scale power plant, which we defined as 500 megawatts (MW) and emitting about 3 millions tons of carbon dioxide (CO_2) annually. We based this definition on some of the key reports we reviewed, which used 500 MW as a standard power plant, and stated that such a plant would emit about 3 million tons of CO_2. Actual CO_2 emissions from a power plant can vary based on a variety of factors, including the

---

[1] EPRI is an independent nonprofit company funded by electricity producers that conducts research and development in the electricity sector. EPRI's work was part of the following report: Global CCS Institute, *Strategic Analysis of the Global Status of Carbon Capture and Storage: Synthesis Report* (Canberra, Australia, 2009).

amount of time that a power plant is operated. We also reviewed available data on the use of key coal technologies compiled by IEA and the Global CCS Institute.

To identify the potential for these technologies to be used commercially in the future along with any associated challenges or implications, we reviewed key reports on CCS and efficiency technologies. We also examined reports developed by DOE, IEA, and electricity industry groups, which lay out goals for the deployment of advanced coal technologies to reduce CO_2 emissions. We also used our interviews with stakeholders with expertise on these technologies to seek their views on the potential challenges to the commercial deployment of these technologies and implications that could be associated with their use.

Finally, we conducted site visits to coal power plants and research facilities in three states—Alabama, Maryland, and West Virginia. We selected this nonprobability sample of states because they contained projects involving advanced coal technologies. During these visits, we interviewed utilities and technology vendors about the goals for these projects along with any challenges they were encountering.

Appendix III: Comments from the Department of Energy

Note: GAO comments supplementing those in the report text appear at the end of this appendix. Page numbers in draft report may differ from those in this report.

Department of Energy
Washington, DC 20585

June 4, 2010

Mr. Mark E. Gaffigan
Director
Natural Resources and Environment Team
U.S. Government Accountability Office
441 G Street, NW, Mail 2T23A
Washington, DC 20548

Dear Mr. Gaffigan:

Thank you for the opportunity to review the Government Accountability Office (GAO) draft report entitled, "Coal Power Plants: Opportunities Exist for DOE to Provide Better Information on the Maturity of Key Technologies to Reduce Carbon Dioxide Emissions" (GAO-10-675). Enclosed pleased find the U.S. Department of Energy's comments on the draft report.

If you have any questions or comments please contact Dr. Darren Mollot of my staff at (301) 903-2700.

Sincerely,

James J. Markowsky
Assistant Secretary
Office of Fossil Energy

Enclosure:
DOE Comments on Draft GAO Report

Printed with soy ink on recycled paper

See comment 1.

See comment 1.

Department of Energy Comments on GAO "Coal Power Plants: Opportunities Exist for DOE to Provide Better Information on the Maturity of Key Technologies to Reduce Carbon Dioxide Emissions (GAO-10-675) (GAO Draft Report)

This responds to your request for comments by the Department of Energy on the above referenced GAO Draft Report.

Our main response is that we agree with GAO's statement that DOE plays a "key role" in working to advance carbon capture and storage (CCS) and efficiency technologies toward commercialization and in helping policy makers have an accurate view of their maturity (pages 3, 14, 53). However, we take some exception with GAO's assessment that DOE is unable to provide a clear picture of the maturity of these technologies or quantify the necessary resources that might be required to move these technologies toward commercial demonstration (this assertion can be found in several places within the report including pages 6, 14, 30, 53).

The Office of Fossil Energy (FE) acknowledged that it could improve upon its current process of providing a clearer picture of technology maturity. FE, working with several national labs, conducts a great deal of research, development, and demonstration activities on CCS and other carbon reduction technologies. These efforts are reported, analyzed, reviewed, and studied, the outcomes from which frequent and continued assessments are made regarding the current status of CCS technologies including their commercial readiness. Included in many of these assessments are specific development timelines that can be used to ascertain how long development will take, and how much development will likely cost. These activities also feed into the development of CCS Roadmaps (e.g. Carbon Sequestration Technology Roadmap and Program Plan http://www.netl.doe.gov/technologies/carbon_seq/refshelf/project%20portfolio/2007/2007Roadmap.pdf,) for the specific development of core CO_2 reduction technologies. These activities and others collectively paint a very accurate picture of the current status of CCS technologies, and provide an excellent gauge on what resources would need to be committed in order to achieve deployment of CCS by the 2020 timeframe.

Furthermore, GAO made the following recommendation beginning on page 14 (also repeated on pages 6-8, and the lower left hand corner of the front cover):

> *"We recommend that the Secretary of Energy direct the Office of Fossil Energy to develop a standard set of benchmarks to gauge the maturity of key technologies and report to Congress on the maturity of these technologies. As part of this process, the Office of Fossil Energy should consider consulting DOE's Technology Readiness Assessment Guide to develop benchmarks and reporting requirements."*

Consistent with our continued efforts to supply policy makers with clear information in a form more amenable for them to gauge the maturity of CCS technologies, we concur with this recommendation. The Office of Fossil Energy will commit to develop a

Corrective Action Plan, and will, at regular intervals, report to Congress on the status of
its actions toward instituting GAO's recommendation.

Specific clarifying comments on the GAO report are as follows:

1 On page 28, the report states:

> *"DOE does not systematically assess the maturity of key coal technologies, but
> we found consensus among stakeholders that CCS is less mature than
> efficiency technologies"*

Although DOE has not assessed the maturity of coal technologies using technology
readiness levels (TRLs), we are very aware of the maturity of all the technologies in the
portfolio. We plan to do a formal TRL assessment in the near future.

See comment 2.

It would also be important to clarify the precise meaning of the term, "efficiency
technologies" in this context. There is a considerable difference between improving
coal plant efficiencies as opposed to more efficient light bulbs

See comment 2.

Furthermore, this is an overly broad statement. For example, one could argue that post-
combustion CO_2 capture via amine scrubbing, plus enhanced oil recovery (EOR) for
CO_2 storage, is much more mature than 1400°F ultrasupercritical "efficiency"
technology.

2 In response to the comments on page 30, we would like to point out that we are
currently in compliance with the policy stated in bullet point #1:

> *"Federal standards for internal control require agency managers to compare
> actual program performance to planned or expected results and analyze
> significant differences"*

See comment 3.

The way this particular set of points is organized gives the appearance that DOE may
not be fulfilling this Federal standard. However, variances are routinely calculated and
analyzed in accordance with these standards.

3 On page 35, the report states that there is:

> *"Only One Integrated CCS Project Operating in a Coal Plant"* and goes on to
> state, *"The only integrated CCS project in a coal plant is the Mountaineer
> Plant in WV according to stakeholders"*

See comment 4.

There is a second integrated CCS project operating in a coal plant. It is the Great Plains
Gasification plant. In this project, the CO_2 is captured and piped to Canada for
Enhanced Oil Recovery (EOR) where it is permanently stored.

4 Page 39 discusses several issues related to efficiency technologies being deployed at new plants:

> *"Most stakeholders considered ultrasupercritical and IGCC plants commercially demonstrated (TRL 9)"*

and

> *"A few stakeholders considered IGCC plants less mature than ultrasupercritical"*

See comment 5.

With respect to both statements, it is necessary to define the Ultrasupercritical (USC) temperatures being discussed here. The Ultrasupercritical term has been used for plants ranging from 1112°F to 1400°F. In addition, the Tampa and Wabash IGCCs are operating commercially today as are other IGCC plants outside the US at TRL=9

5 The information presented on page 40 is potentially misleading as it attempts to compare the commercial deployability of CCS versus efficiency technologies.

See comment 6.

Efficiency improvements may give a few percentage points of improvement resulting in perhaps 10% reduction in CO_2 emissions, whereas commercial deployment of CCS could result in 90% or greater CO_2 reductions. Also, CCS should be deployable by 2020. Moreover, CCS can be considered to be essentially deployable today with IGCC plus EOR, albeit with additional integration risks and financial incentive to do so. In summary, while the information on page 40 is accurate from a certain point of view, the perspective infers that the two approaches can be easily compared whereas the scope and benefits of the two approaches are very different.

6. Page 48 summarizes the positive and negative implications of using CCS versus efficiency technologies. With respect to the advantages of using plant efficiency improvements, the following statement is made:

> *"A key advantage is that plant efficiency improvements offer more potential for near term emissions reductions"*

See comment 6.

While this statement may be technically true, it is important to note that there is far less potential to achieve the deep CO_2 reductions that will be needed to meet our nation's climate-related goals solely using efficiency technologies. It is important to have that in mind when making these kinds of general statements.

7. On page 50, the report states:

> *"DOE has raised concerns about CCS water consumption"*

See comment 7.

"DOE estimated that post-combustion capture technology could almost double water consumption at a coal plant, while pre-combustion capture would increase water use by 37%"

While this is true, it should also be mentioned that the continued development of advanced CCS and cooling technologies could significantly reduce water use for CCS.

See comment 8.

8. While the information presented on page 22 is factually correct concerning existing coal plants, it is important to note that in 2008, the U.S. coal-fired power plant (CFPP) fleet had a generation-weighted average efficiency of 32.5% while the top ten percent of the fleet had an efficiency of 37.6%, five percentage points higher. (http://www.netl.doe.gov/energy-analyses/pubs/ImpCFPPGHGRdctns_0410.pdf) Furthermore, "Ultra-supercritical steam parameters of 4350 psi and 1112°F (300 bar and 600°C) are in operation today with generating efficiencies of 40% (HHV). There are several years of experience with these plants in Europe and Japan, with excellent availability, and plans have been announced for several USC PC plants in the United States." http://mydocs.epri.com/docs/public/000000000001016877.pdf [see pages 3-5]

See comment 8.

Future plants could go much higher in efficiency using USC with 1400°F steam temps or IGCC with solid oxide fuel cells 9. With respect to the assertion on page 46 that advanced ultrasupercritical plants requiring metal alloys that withstand 27% higher steam temperatures, we recommend that absolute temperatures are used. A percent increase in temperature value is only meaningful if you use <u>absolute</u> temperatures (Rankine or Kelvin). To advance from 1116°F to 1300°F using absolute temperatures would be a 12% increase in temperature and going further to 1400°F would be an 18% increase. Under the circumstances, it might be better to just say "a temperature increase of 300°F to 400°F."

The following are GAO's comments on the Department of Energy's letter
dated June 4, 2010.

GAO Comments

1. We acknowledge that DOE publishes reports that assess the technical
and economic feasibility of some advanced coal technologies and revised
our report accordingly. While some of these reports provide valuable
information, we found that the agency does not systematically review
these technologies, have a standard set of benchmarks to describe the
maturity of technologies as they progress to commercialization, or prepare
a formal report on a regular basis to assess their maturity or the resources
needed to advance technologies toward commercialization. We are
encouraged that DOE acknowledges that improvements can be made to
the information it provides to policymakers and concurs with our
recommendation that the agency develop a standard set of benchmarks
and report on the maturity of these technologies to Congress. Finally, the
agency notes that it plans to do a formal assessment using TRLs of coal
technologies in the near future in line with our recommendation.

2. Our draft report defines efficiency technologies as referring to new
power plant designs such as Integrated Gasification Combined Cycle and
ultrasupercritical along with efficiency upgrades made to existing coal
power plants. The statement in our draft report that CCS is less mature
than efficiency technologies in coal power plants is based on stakeholder
views of coal technologies using our TRL scale. Our draft report notes that
certain aspects of CCS have been used commercially in other industries
such as natural gas processing or enhanced oil recovery. In addition, the
draft report indicates that one of the challenges to using advanced
ultrasupercritical plants is the lack of metal alloys to withstand increased
steam temperatures.

3. We are not suggesting that DOE is not complying with this standard.
This standard outlines the broad duties federal agencies have in managing
their programs. Our finding discussed in our comment one above identifies
that DOE could do more to improve its efforts to address this standard.

4. We have revised our draft report to indicate that there is only one
integrated CCS project in a coal power plant. DOE states that the Great
Plains Synfuels plant is an integrated CCS project. We agree that this plant
is capturing and transporting CO_2 to be used as part of enhanced oil
recovery in Canada's Weyburn oil field. However, this plant gasifies coal in
order to make synthetic natural gas; it is not a coal power plant that
produces electricity, which is the focus of our report.

5. Our report defines ultrasupercritical plants as having steam temperatures of about 1,100 degrees Fahrenheit.

6. We agree with DOE that there is a difference in the ability for CCS and efficiency technologies to achieve reductions in CO_2 emissions from coal power plants. Specifically, our report states that the use of efficiency technologies by themselves are "unlikely to meet ambitious cuts in CO_2." In addition, we state that efficiency technologies cannot reduce CO_2 emissions from the same extent as CCS. For example, we state that an ultrasupercritical plant emits about one-third less CO_2 than an average coal power plant in the United States, while CCS offers the potential to capture 90 percent of a plant's CO_2 emissions.

7. We revised our draft report to note that advancements in CCS and cooling technologies could help to reduce water use for CCS. In addition, it is important to note that our report states that pre-combustion capture could increase water use by 73 percent, not 37 percent as DOE's comment indicates.

8. We have made these technical changes to our draft report. It is important to note that we state that advanced materials are needed to withstand temperature increases of 300 to 500 degrees Fahrenheit. This is because today's ultrasupercritical plants have steam temperatures of about 1,100 degrees Fahrenheit, while DOE has set goals to develop materials to withstand steam temperatures of 1,400 to 1,600 degrees Fahrenheit.

Appendix IV: GAO Contact and Staff Acknowledgments

GAO Contact	Mark Gaffigan, (202) 512-3841 or gaffiganm@gao.gov
Staff Acknowledgments	In addition to the contact names above, key contributors to this report included Jon Ludwigson (Assistant Director), Chloe Brown, Scott Heacock, Alison O'Neill, Kiki Theodoropoulos, and Jarrod West. Important assistance was also provided by Chuck Bausell, Nirmal Chaudhary, Cindy Gilbert, Madhav Panwar, and Jeanette Soares.